THE
Sacred
Rules
OF MANAGEMENT

*How to Get Control
of Your Time and
Your Work*

STANLEY E. SMITH

VanderWyk & Burnham
Acton, Massachusetts

Copyright © 1997 by Stanley E. Smith

 Published by VanderWyk & Burnham
A Division of Publicom, Inc.
P.O. Box 2789, Acton, Massachusetts 01720

This book is available for quantity purchases. For information on bulk discounts, call (800) 789-7916 or write to Special Sales at the above address.

Library of Congress Cataloging-in-Publication Data
Smith, Stan (Stanley E.)
   The sacred rules of management: how to get control of your time and your work / Stanley Edson Smith.
      p.   cm.
   Includes index.
   ISBN: 0-9641089-7-6
   1. Management. 2. Time management. 3. Success in business. 4. Strategic planning. I. Title.
HD31.S595   1997
650.1—dc21
                                                            96-51965
                                                                 CIP

Book design by Margaret Ong Tsao

Manufactured in the United States of America
10 9 8 7 6 5 4 3 2 1

To a truly effective manager (and a great dad)

Peter W. Smith

Contents

Introduction

This small work was written partly out of protest and partly from a wish to contribute something toward the renewal of American managerial effectiveness.

Since acquiring an M.B.A. from Cornell, I have spent several years working at staff and middle management positions in banking, publishing, and government. In each of these fields I have been privileged to observe some very able managers, but also amused and chagrined to observe some breathtakingly bad ones (including some enjoying lofty titles and hefty paychecks).

Now, no manager is perfect, and even the worst managers have redeeming qualities. Certainly I acknowledge my own flaws and limitations as a manager and as a judge of others. It has seemed to me, though, that even the most senior managers (through habit or in pursuit of the latest management fad) impair their effectiveness by occasionally violating the most elementary principles of management, principles that would be included in any book of elementary rules for managers.

The trouble is that no such book has existed. Bookstore shelves groan, of course, with books on "management," and many of them are very good. Too many of them, however, are simply case studies of particular companies or industries, or treatises on a current management theory. None gives a clear, concise set of basic rules of management that can serve as a guide for new managers and a reminder for experienced ones. This book endeavors to fill that gap.

Managers in all fields of activity must manage time, paperwork, projects, and people to carry out their responsibilities and get things done. This book lists and discusses some basic rules for managing these resources, both inside the office and—to the large extent that a well-managed and balanced life is important—outside it.

The demands of a busy life may make it impossible to use every day all the specific techniques discussed here. Some of these techniques will be more important to your work than others at different times. Understanding the principles discussed here will help you as a manager to make the right choices under the circumstances you face in your work.

Many of these rules will seem obvious. That's quite all right. Sometimes the truth that is right in front of our noses is the most difficult to see. With this book I hope to remind new and experienced managers alike of a few "obvious" truths and thereby increase their effectiveness.

The Sacred Rules of Management

Managing Your

DAY

PLAN YOUR DAY, AND PUT YOUR PLAN ON PAPER.

---

1 Write down a schedule for your day.

Regularly each day, either early in the morning or in the evening, write down a schedule for the upcoming day. This schedule, or list of events, should include at least all special events scheduled for a particular time. Unplanned meetings or other events can be added as they arise. If you like, you can also include routine events such as meals and morning and afternoon work periods, at least for the satisfaction of checking them off when you finish them.

Writing down your schedule takes only a few minutes and prevents your worrying about forgetting an appointment. Doing this even on Saturdays helps you to get the most out of your weekend. If you keep a daily diary or journal, your written schedule can be a useful record of events you want to write about.

2 Include some prime working time and some quiet time in your schedule.

You have a peak-performance, or prime, time each day when you are at your best and most alert. For many, if not for most people, this time is in the morning. Find out when your prime time is, and try to schedule a large block of that time each day to do your most important work.

You should also schedule some quiet time each day, time when you can be relatively free of noise, visitors, phone calls, and other interruptions or disturbances. Use this time for quiet reading or reflection. These activities are necessary for a full life, but in these busy times filled with technological and other diversions, quiet time seldom arises on its own. It must be planned and defended. The early morning or the evening is usually best for this, but your lunch break or other times can serve the purpose.

If you can arrange for some quiet time at the office as well, to attend to important paperwork or to think, you should do so.

3 Write down a Things to Do list for your day.

Your other daily list should be a list of tasks you intend to accomplish that day. This list should be drawn from your calendar and from a list of weekly goals, but other items can be added as they arise day to day. You should also include tasks postponed or left unfinished from the previous day.

These tasks should be listed in the order of their importance, giving due allowance for their urgency. Do not ignore important tasks that are not urgent. Tasks that arise in the course of the day can be added in their proper places. Setting priorities is essential to efficient time management. If there isn't time to do everything on your list, then deciding and understanding your priorities will at least let you make the best use of the time you have.

If your job isn't your entire life (and it shouldn't be), keep separate schedules and Things to Do lists for your day as a whole and for your day at the office.

4 Work your way down each list in order, checking off each event or task as you complete it.

Start with the first item on the list, and work on it until you complete it, have gone as far with it as you can at that time, or are otherwise obliged to put it aside. If you have completed it, check it off. Then move on to the next item on the list.

Using your schedule and your Things to Do list enables you to get through the day in an orderly and organized manner. Nothing is forgotten or neglected; the most important tasks are accomplished first, to the extent possible; and you gain a sense of momentum and achievement as you check items off and move down your list.

5 Keep an appointment calendar, lists of goals, and a Reminder File.

Note your appointments, and other events scheduled for a particular day and time, in an appointment calendar, which you should consult each day when you prepare your schedule. Your daily Things to Do list should be drawn from this and from a list of goals or tasks for the week, which should itself be drawn from similar lists for the month and the year. (Goals lists are described further in Rules 36–40.) The best and most practical method of getting what you want out of life is to keep long-term lists of goals, regularly review them, and translate them into short-term tasks (action steps toward your goals).

Another useful tool to use in preparing your daily Things to Do list is a Reminder File. This file contains a folder for each day of the month and for each month. Into these folders can be put notes and documents (usually reminders and follow-up papers) that you want to review on a particular day, either in the current month or later. At the start of each month, put the documents for that month into the daily folders. By checking the day's folder each day, you can see any paperwork you had put aside for that day and note the appropriate task on your Things to Do list.

6 Follow a regular schedule on weekdays.

If your daily schedule is balanced and reasonable, then working, sleeping, eating, exercising, and relaxing at the same time each day enhance your health, your sense of stability, and your productivity. The power of habit, when put to use, reinforces each activity. A regular schedule and familiar surroundings for work help you concentrate. Regular habits save the time otherwise taken to decide about routine matters. They also free your mind for interesting and creative pursuits. As another benefit, relatives and colleagues who know your routine know when it is convenient—or inconvenient—to call or meet with you.

Your schedule preserves the basic structure and balance of your day. Sticking with it is worth a little trouble, even that of postponing a few unfinished tasks at the end of a scheduled work period.

7 Keep a time log occasionally.

At least every few months, choose one day and keep a careful log of how you actually spend your time during that day. Update the log every hour or so, and account for every fifteen minutes. This will allow you to compare how you think you spend your time with how you actually do spend your time.

The results may surprise you. You may be spending more time than you thought on trivial matters. If so, review your priorities and see if there are ways you can prune your schedule to spend more time on what is important.

GET THROUGH THE ROUTINE CHORES OF THE DAY QUICKLY AND EFFICIENTLY.

---

8 Reduce your commuting time as much as possible, and put it to good use.

Commuting to work can be crowded, polluting, dangerous, and very time-consuming. For someone who must drive or ride a long distance to work each day, the cumulative loss of time in a year can be staggering.

At least be aware of this when choosing where to live and where to work. The lack of commuting is one of the greatest advantages of working from home. If you must drive to the office, as most of us must, take the quickest route (which is not necessarily the shortest) and use off-peak hours if you can. Working a second or third shift, or taking advantage of flexible time if your company offers it, can help you avoid crowds.

If you can take public transportation to the office, do so. Not only does it cut down on vehicular pollution, it also frees you to read or think. If you must drive, use the time to reflect on a particular problem, or listen to an educational or musical cassette tape.

9 Consolidate your routine chores.

Doing routine chores, either at or away from the office, one after another in a single block of time is generally the most efficient way of disposing of them. Your mind gets into a pattern of reviewing and accomplishing these chores quickly.

10 Do chores and errands at unusual times.

Try to avoid doing your chores and errands at the same time as everyone else. This will save you much time and inconvenience. If your work schedule allows you to do your shopping during a weekday, do that. Automated teller machines and supermarkets enable you to do your banking and food shopping at odd times. Try to avoid doing errands on Saturday afternoons, since many places of business are busy and crowded then.

11 Consolidate your errands into a single trip.

Trips can consume much time, so organize your tasks to make as few trips as possible (not including pleasure trips, of course). Arrange the shortest route that covers all the necessary stops, and do your errands in the order in which their locations are reached along the route. Again, making your errands trip at an odd hour can save travel and waiting time.

If you have an appointment to which you must travel, confirm the appointment just before you leave. The appointment may have been postponed or canceled without your being notified. Checking first can save you much time and annoyance.

12 Take advantage of pockets of available time.

In the course of even the best-planned day, pockets of time arise during which, if unprepared, you have little to do but twiddle your thumbs and wait. Such moments usually arise when waiting in line at a store or in an office for an appointment, or when traveling.

Use that time to read, think, or make notes, either in pursuit of your goals or simply to relax. A few minutes of reading may not seem like much progress, but as the old saying goes, "Little strokes fell great oaks." Carry with you some reading matter and a notepad, or even a dictation device.

TAKE CARE OF YOUR HEALTH FOR A FULL LIFE.

---

13 Eat sensibly.

A balanced diet is necessary for good health, which is necessary for living a full life and for being as effective a manager as you can be. Good eating habits give you health and energy, and prevent or eliminate obesity, which can drain your energy, endanger your heart, and hurt your appearance.

Eat a good, healthful breakfast, not just a cup of coffee. Have a light lunch. A heavy lunch takes time and contributes to afternoon torpor. In the evening, enjoy a moderate dinner, preferably with family or friends. Good nutritional guidebooks abound; become acquainted with at least one.

14 Don't drink alcohol during the working day.

Drinking alcohol at lunch or at other times during the working day gives you needless calories and may impair your judgment. Letting your boss or a client smell alcohol on your breath doesn't do great things for your professional image, either.

15 Exercise regularly.

This is another of the fundamentals of good health. Exercise helps you to control your weight, improves your muscle tone, improves your circulation, and provides a healthful outlet for stress and tension. Exercising daily or three or four times a week is much better than exercising sporadically or only on weekends. The "weekend-only athlete" is more prone to injury and to strain on the heart, the muscles, and the joints.

Brisk walking is one of the best exercises, especially when combined with a moderate program of calisthenics to strengthen the upper body. Walking benefits your muscles and your cardiovascular system, and it rarely leads to injury. It can thus be enjoyed at any age. Walking can also be incorporated into your daily activities: You can climb the stairs instead of taking the elevator, or walk a short distance to do an errand instead of driving there.

Taking a brisk walk at lunchtime is very beneficial. Getting some fresh air and sunshine is refreshing, and the exercise helps you shed any tension or stress that has built up during the morning. Thus, a brisk walk prepares you for the afternoon. You can even read while you walk, as long as you are a little careful about where you are going and have good peripheral vision. Be careful not to work up a sweat, though, unless a shower and a change of clothes are available when you return.

Participating regularly in amateur sports is a fun way to get exercise. Just be sure to play a sport that is consistent with your age and your level of fitness.

Don't persuade yourself that you have no time for something as fundamentally important as exercise.

16 Take an afternoon nap.

One of the best ways to enhance your productivity is to take an afternoon nap. Midafternoon fatigue is a natural part of the circadian rhythm, and a refreshing sleep break around that time can enhance the quality and number of your waking and working hours.

All too common is the foolish attitude that napping is proper only for babies and the very old, and that anyone else who naps is slothful. Throughout history, many of the world's busiest and most productive people have napped every afternoon. They have found naps to be an indispensable part of a full and vigorous life.

Of course, not all of us have the sort of accommodations and control over our schedule that make napping easy. Nonetheless, it is often possible to doze in a parked car at lunchtime or to take a nap at home before dinner. At least you can take short breaks at work before fatigue builds up. Rest your eyes occasionally, as they consume a surprising amount of nervous energy.

If you can arrange to take a regular nap, though, do yourself a favor and take it. The wisdom of napping should no longer be a well-kept secret.

17 Get enough sleep at night.

When the demands on your time get tight, you will be tempted to cut back on your sleep at night. Resist the temptation. You need to be at your best especially when time is tight, and skimping on sleep impairs your concentration, judgment, and reaction time. If the deprivation is severe enough, you may even risk falling asleep while driving, the consequences of which can be fatal.

The amount of sleep needed to be at one's best varies by individual. You can discover your optimal amount by experimenting—adding or taking away half an hour for a few days at a time until you find the amount of sleep that lets you perform at your peak. Of course, if you take a nap during the day, as recommended in Rule 16, the amount of sleep you need at night will be less.

LEAD A BALANCED LIFE.

18 Limit your vocational work to eight hours a day.

Leave time in your day and in your life for interests and activities outside the office. You owe this to your family or to your friends. You also owe it to yourself. No one should become consumed by a job or a company; earning a living is an important part of life, but not the only important part. You should spend time with loved ones and with the more creative sides of yourself.

Routinely working excessively long hours can ultimately detract from your contribution at work as well. Long hours lead to fatigue, which impairs concentration, judgment, and the creation of fresh ideas. If sustained, long hours lead to staleness and burnout. Workaholics make the critical mistakes of seeking perfection instead of excellence, developing a martyr complex, mistaking activity for achievement, alienating their family and friends, and allowing their other interests and skills to atrophy.

There are emergency times, of course, when long hours are necessary. If such periods go on for weeks or months, however, you should realize that there is a chronic problem either with your work habits or with your job requirements. One or the other should be changed. You owe a good and full day's work to your employer, but not your whole life.

19 Spend time with your family and friends.

Good personal relationships are vitally important to leading a happy life, and they need to be nurtured. Don't let your spouse gradually become a stranger. Be part of your children's growing up, for otherwise they will be grown and gone before you know it.

Good friends, especially those of long standing, are precious, so keep in touch with them, at least annually. Keep acquiring new friends as well.

20 Cultivate outside interests and hobbies.

The cultivation of interests and hobbies outside the office is not frivolous; it is necessary. Interests and hobbies outside the office help you develop the full range of your intellect and abilities, give rest and refreshing change to the brain, and make you a more interesting person.

Having a hobby that uses different skills from those you use at work gives you the best rest and relief. If you sit at a desk and read and write all day, for example, try to find a hobby that engages physical or nonverbal skills, or that requires eye-hand coordination. Excellent examples include art (drawing, painting, photography), music (piano, violin, guitar), sports (golf, tennis), and strategy games (chess).

If you lose your job, a hobby can cushion the blow by giving you something enjoyable to do and by providing a sense of continuity to your life. It also helps you to preserve your sense of self, which can be badly damaged if you have identified yourself too closely or entirely with the job.

21 Plan your weekend—and stay away from your office.

The two-day weekend is a fairly recent invention of civilization and one of the best. It gives structure and balance to the week. Protecting your weekend from office work gives you time (a) to do necessary household chores, which are often relegated to the weekend, especially when both adults in a household have jobs, and (b) to develop your outside relationships and interests (not to mention just plain resting!). You can then return to the office on Monday feeling refreshed.

To make the most of your weekend, you should plan it. Draw up a schedule or at least a Things to Do list. Get the necessary chores out of the way as quickly as possible and then do some planned fun activities: reading, playing with your kids, riding a bike with your spouse. Indulge in your hobby. Allow time just to sit around and relax, but don't let your whole weekend slip by that way. By doing a little planning you can avoid spending the whole weekend either working at chores or being a couch potato.

Managing Your

PAPERWORK

*DO BUSINESS
IN WRITING.*

22 Keep notes of ideas, conversations, and decisions.

Memories can be faulty. The spoken word disappears into the air, but writing endures. One of the best habits you can acquire to be effective at the office is that of taking notes on business conversations, decisions, and ideas. In that way they can be retained, communicated, and acted upon.

Do your thinking on paper. You may be surprised how closely related the processes of thinking and writing are, and how they support and develop each other as you progress. Having a paper trail of your thinking process allows you to review it and your resulting decisions.

Decisions reached at the end of a meeting or a conversation can easily be forgotten unless they are reiterated in writing. Preparing a memo of a decision forces the writer to be organized and precise in thought and expression, and forces the recipient to be accountable for agreeing with or disputing the decision and for carrying it out.

23 Date your documents.

Noting the date on any document you receive or create, even a sheet of notes, is a useful habit. It preserves the historical record, which is often needed to obtain information or to follow the progress of an event or a decision. The importance of a document can be determined more easily later if its date is known.

24 Always have a notepad handy.

Always have a notepad within reach so that you can jot down an idea or a task as it occurs to you or as it is brought to your attention. At the office, keep a notepad on your desktop and carry one with you when you leave your desk. At home, keep a notepad and a pen or pencil by the phone, by your favorite chair, and by your bedside. If a brilliant idea strikes at 3:00 A.M., you should be able to write it down.

MAKE GOOD USE OF FILE FOLDERS.

---

25 Keep lists of projects instead of piles of paper.

Keep a Projects List at the office, and as each new project is assigned to you, add it to the list. Note the date the project is assigned and its deadline. When you complete a project, check or cross it off the list. This Projects List should be an important source for your daily Things to Do list.

26 Keep a file for each project or job-related subject.

If a project is more than a one-day job, create a manila folder file for it. Write the title of the project on the flap, and keep all documents related to that project in the file. (These suggestions can be applied to electronic files and folders as well.) Keep the project file in your desk (or on your disk) or on a current-projects shelf within easy reach.

Project files are active only for the duration of the projects. You should also keep permanent files for those subjects that are related to your work and on which you need to collect information, for example, regular financial reports and the workings of other departments and committees. Related files can be conveniently grouped together in file pockets.

While files for current projects or relevant subjects should be kept within easy reach, inactive files, such as for completed projects, should be stored out of the way. If you find that papers are starting to pile up on a corner of your desk, review them, discard or forward those you can, and put the rest in the appropriate project files. In this way all your papers will be either filed or on your desk being worked on.

Only one person—either yourself or an assistant—should organize and manage your files. That is one area in which, surely, "too many cooks spoil the broth."

27 Clear your desk of all papers except those you are working on at the moment.

A cluttered desk, piled high with papers of all sorts, is tolerable to some, but it is needlessly distracting and usually a sign of disorganization or sloth. The mind can concentrate on only one matter at a time, so when working on a task you should get out the papers related to that task and put all others away. An effective filing system, such as the one just described, enables you to do this without losing track of anything. Piles are poor substitutes for orderly files.

Clutter on a desk can make you feel overwhelmed and buried under an avalanche of tasks. This can cause anxiety and lead to ulcers or worse disabilities. Be a "clean-desk executive." Don't cover your desk with a lot of personal photographs, souvenirs, or knickknacks, either. These take up useful desk space and can be distracting. Except perhaps for one or two items, keep such things on a side shelf, or at home.

At the end of the day, clear all papers off your desk. This will give you a fresh start the next morning.

28 When you complete a project, purge and relocate its file.

Once a project is done and its file is therefore no longer active, take a few minutes to discard any duplicate or clearly useless papers. Keep the rest, in case you need to refer to the project again. Replace all paper clips with staples: Staples are more expendable, and they don't get tangled as clips can. Then note the completion date on the file and put it among your inactive files. In this way you can refer to the paperwork related to the project later if you need to, but the file will not be in the way of your active files.

29 Periodically conduct a major purge of your files.

Twice a year or so, review the manila and computer files you still have and discard those that you clearly no longer need. Make sure any remaining inactive files are separated from active ones. Go through your subject files, which are usually kept indefinitely, and discard unneeded documents. This exercise can save you much file space and needless headaches later when looking for old documents.

LEARN TO PROCESS YOUR INCOMING PAPERWORK EFFICIENTLY.

---

30 Sort through your in-box two or three times a day.

Don't drop everything every time someone drops a piece of paper in your in-box. This causes too many interruptions. Let the papers accumulate for a few hours while you work on your current projects. Going through your in-box two or three times a day (morning, midday, and midafternoon, for instance) will let you stay on top of incoming paperwork as well as your Things to Do list.

31 Sort through your in-box efficiently.

When you sort through your in-box, examine one document at a time. If it can be discarded, forwarded, or filed without requiring further action, do that immediately. If you can act upon it and dispose of it quickly (say, by dashing off a note or by making a call), do so. If the document will require lengthy reading, put it in a Pending Reading file for later attention.

If the paper requires further action that will take more than a minute, note the action on your Things to Do list and put the document in the appropriate project file or in your Reminder File. Once you have sorted through and emptied your in-box, return to work on your (now possibly revised) Things to Do list.

32 Reply promptly to memos and letters.

Whenever possible, when you receive a memo or a letter that requires a reply, write your reply right on the document, make a copy for yourself, and return the document to the sender.

If you have to write a long memo or letter, avoid writing in longhand. Using a word processor (if you can type, which you should know how to do) or a dictation device is faster. Before dictating a long document, first prepare a rough outline or at least a list of the points you want to make, and refer to it as you dictate. The first draft of a dictated document is usually somewhat disjointed and needlessly wordy, so edit the draft carefully for grammar, logic, and conciseness.

Communicating in writing gives the recipient a chance to prepare and deliver a thoughtful response. In all your writing, take care to be clear, logical, and concise.

ORGANIZE YOUR READING AND REFERENCE MATERIAL.

33 Keep your reference material in an appropriately labeled file folder or a binder.

Reference material can be kept in the related subject file or, if the material is more general in scope, in a file or binder of its own. Keep it in your desk or on a convenient shelf. Also maintain a list or a visual display of all your reference materials for quick referral.

34 Keep a file of your reading matter.

Keep material you intend to read in a separate, temporary folder. If this Pending Reading file tends to get thick, keep a list of its contents for easy reference.

35 Schedule regular reading time.

Schedule some regular time for yourself, every day or at least every week, to catch up on your reading. Consolidate as much of your reading as you can for that time. Scheduling a regular reading time rather than relying entirely on spare moments can be a great help in keeping up with your professional reading. Remember to make time to read for pleasure and for self-education as well.

Managing Your

PROJECTS

GET YOUR GOALS DOWN ON PAPER.

36 List your long-term personal and professional goals.

Some projects are assigned or otherwise imposed on you. Other projects, usually your most important ones, are derived from your own personal and professional goals. You must therefore determine your goals and get them down on paper. Working toward your own defined goals adds purpose, meaning, and direction to your life.

Keep your lists of personal goals separate from your lists of professional ones. Your job is a big enough part of your life to have its own lists, but it isn't your whole life.

37 Make your goals specific and concrete, and rank them.

Instead of "Get rich" or "Be happy," list specific goals such as (for instance) "Achieve a net worth of $X" and "Climb the

Matterhorn." Try brainstorming a list first, jotting down whatever appeals to you, and then winnow out the goals that you're not willing to work for. Make the remaining goals specific, and rank them in their order of importance to you.

Set your priorities and decide which goals mean the most to you. If you bear them in mind as you go about your daily activities, you will move toward those goals in often unexpected ways.

38 Treat each goal as a project.

To start changing your goals into reality, regard each goal as a project and prepare a list of the actions that will need to be taken to achieve the goal. (This process is discussed more fully in Rule 44.)

39 Review your goals periodically.

As life goes on, needs and priorities change, and goals change accordingly. Some goals are added, and others are revised or dropped. To keep your goals lists current with your life, review the lists periodically and make any necessary revisions.

40 List goals for each year, month, week, and day.

Preparing lists of goals and their action steps for the year, the month, the week, and the day is the best way to break your dream goals into manageable pieces, as well as to keep track of the more mundane chores of life. Your list of Things to Do This Week can include "Take three two-mile walks" (in pursuit of your goal of physical fitness), "Read Lincoln's First Inaugural Address" (in pursuit of an educational goal), and "Take trash to transfer station" (a routine chore but actually in pursuit of a goal of good home maintenance).

Derive each list from your longer-range lists and from your appointment calendar. Review your yearly goals each month and your monthly goals each week, and make additions or deletions as appropriate. Try to accomplish each task as early as possible in each time period: It's much easier to get ahead and then coast than to start slowly and catch up later. At least on the weekly list, note which day you plan to accomplish each task. Use a "D" for the tasks you do each day (such as sorting the mail).

USE LISTS AND NOTES TO ORGANIZE AND KEEP TRACK OF PROJECTS AT THE OFFICE.

41 Keep a prioritized, running list of current projects.

A project is a task large or complex enough to require more than a day of work. Lesser tasks can be relegated directly to your list of Things to Do Today or This Week.

At the office, keep a running list of current projects, including both those assigned to you and those you assign to yourself to achieve your professional goals. Add each project and its date of assignment as it is assigned, and check or cross off each project as you complete it.

Use some system for rating projects in their order of importance (A, B, C; or stars), allowing for their urgency (U). Then work on your projects in their proper order.

42 Eliminate projects that do not belong to you.

Some projects are imposed on you whether you like them or not. Others may be offered to you that don't further your goals. Say "no" tactfully to those. If you accept a project and later find that, because of a change in goals or priorities, it is no longer worth your time, get rid of it if you can by delegating it, reassigning it, or simply letting it drop. Eliminating time-wasting projects streamlines your activities and keeps your effectiveness at its peak.

43 Write a summary of each project you take on.

When you take on a reasonably large or complex project, create a Project Summary page for it. On that page, concisely describe the project, including its purpose, its scope (or limits), its deadline, and other pertinent details. This summary will be very helpful as you organize the project. Keep it in your project file.

44 Prepare a Project Steps list.

Your first step in organizing a project is to list all the steps, or actions, you or others must take to complete the project and to follow up on it properly. If others will be involved in the project, get them involved in preparing this list. Do some brainstorming and list all the steps you can think of as they occur to you. Consider all the factors of the project: time, material, personnel, even politics.

Once all the steps are on paper, arrange them in order of action. The outline format is ideal for large projects, as it visually distinguishes various stages of the project from each other. Also incorporate intermediate goals and deadlines into your list. Review the list with your boss and any involved colleagues or staff, and make revisions as needed.

Keep this Project Steps list, as well as your Project Summary (Rule 43), notes of project ideas, and related documents, in your project file.

45 Work you way down the list of Project Steps.

Once your Project Steps list is ready, work your way down it. Complete one step at a time, and check off each step as you complete it.

Respect the project deadlines, and if you think you will miss a deadline, inform your boss in writing ahead of time. If others are responsible for completing some of the steps, keep track of their progress. Measure progress on the project by achievement, not by mere activity.

To sharpen your incentive, reward yourself for reaching intermediate goals and for completing the project. When you have completed the project, tell your boss.

MANAGE YOUR PROJECT TIME WELL.

46 Develop your powers of concentration.

One of the most useful skills you can develop is that of concentration—of focusing your attention on the matter to which you have directed your attention and excluding all distractions from your mind. This ability (also known as mental discipline) is not a gift you must be born with; it is a skill that almost anyone can develop through practice.

Perseverance is the key to developing this skill to its fullest. Select an item for your attention, and concentrate on that item. When your mind starts to wander from it, as it inevitably will at first, firmly return it to the matter at hand. You may have to do this repeatedly, but don't despair. Keep at it, and you will develop the ability to get the most mental work done in the least amount of time you can.

When working on a project, concentrate on one step at a time. When that step is done, put it from your mind and move on to the next one.

47 Allocate enough time to complete the project on schedule.

Allow yourself and others involved in a project enough time to complete it. Recognize (a) that time is a necessary project resource and (b) that the time needed for a project can be difficult to estimate accurately. Allocate an extra margin of time to your estimate, therefore, to accommodate setbacks and unexpected problems.

48 Schedule reasonably long, uninterrupted blocks of time to work on important projects.

Concentrating your time as well as your attention enhances your effectiveness. Working during a solid block of time enables you to acquire momentum and keeps you from having to reorient yourself to the task after an interruption.

Work on important projects during the hours when you are at your best and most alert. For most people these hours are in the morning. During this most productive period, discourage interruptions by closing your door, or by instructing your secretary (if you have one) to fend off visitors and calls, or by hiding yourself in a conference room, in a library, or at home. Discourage "drop-in" visits by putting up a sign or letting your colleagues know in advance that you are busy.

When working on a project, have all necessary papers and other materials at hand so you won't have to waste valuable time looking for them. Your project file (see Rule 26) is very helpful for this purpose.

49 When traveling, take books or project papers with you.

Although long blocks of work time are best, you can also make progress toward your goals during the gaps of time that arise while traveling if you take work materials with you. You may be able to get some reading done in trains, planes, and cars (if you're not driving!). If you can't read in a moving vehicle, keep a dictation device handy to capture thoughts and ideas.

50 Try to finish projects just in time— on time, but not by much.

Do meet your deadlines. Other people very likely depend on your getting your work done on time. Try not to be greatly in advance of your deadlines, however, since your results in that case may be less up-to-date or in some other way less useful.

MAKE NOTES ON YOUR COMPLETED PROJECTS.

---

51 Keep an Achievements List of professional accomplishments.

Keep a list of your professional achievements, including honors and completed important projects. We too often forget or ignore these. Review and update your Achievements List regularly. Such a list is good for your morale and sharpens your incentive to achieve. It is also useful during performance evaluations, when asking for a raise, and if, by choice or necessity, you find yourself applying for another job.

52 **If the completed project will recur, note and file any lessons you learned in completing it.**

Few large projects go completely the way you expect them to go the first time. If the lessons learned are not jotted down, however, they may be forgotten by the time the project comes up again. Write them down and put them in the project file. You may even want to revise your Project Steps list. There is no better way to avoid repeating mistakes and to ensure a smooth completion of the project the next time.

If the project was one of handling a crisis that could recur, analyze the crisis to see how it might have been prevented or handled better. Then note and implement the appropriate steps.

MEET CRISES CALMLY AND DIRECTLY.

53 **When a crisis arises, stay calm and think the problem through.**

Nothing is accomplished by panicking. In almost any crisis (other than a physical emergency), a few minutes or even a few hours can be taken to think through the problem and jot down some notes on its essential features and some possible solutions and their consequences. If you need more time and can somehow "buy" that time, do so. Then organize and implement a plan of action. Acting on a conscious decision is almost always better than drifting.

54 Sleep on important decisions.

Getting a night's sleep before making an important decision gives your subconscious a chance to work on the decision. A new solution, or at least a new facet of the problem, may be apparent in the morning, and the final decision will be made by a rested mind. Waiting overnight before checking and sending an important document can be a wise precaution as well.

55 Don't procrastinate.

Procrastination is perhaps the greatest time-waster of all. Don't put off a possibly unpleasant task for no good reason. Develop the habit of completing tasks promptly for the satisfaction of having accomplished them. If necessary, subdivide your Project Steps into minitasks that can be completed quickly, and make progress by taking smaller steps at a time. Drawing up comparative lists of the advantages and disadvantages of completing a task can help put it and your proposed delay in their proper perspective.

Managing Your

MEETINGS

CHOOSE YOUR MEETINGS CAREFULLY.

56 Avoid **unnecessary meetings.**

The mania for meetings is a bane of office life. Many managers foolishly believe that the more meetings they attend, the more important they are. In fact, relatively few meetings are truly productive. There are no greater time-wasters than poorly run meetings or meetings that need not be held at all, since the wasted time is multiplied by the number of people at the meeting.

If you can communicate by phone, memo, or electronic mail rather than by calling a meeting, do so. If you can reasonably have someone on your staff attend a meeting in your place, do that. Business travel costs much time and money, so if the participants in a proposed meeting are far apart, arrange a conference call instead of a meeting if you can.

57 Don't meet for a meal to discuss business.

Sharing a meal with a business colleague to get better acquainted or to chat is fine. Such occasions are mainly social. You should not, however, combine a meal with a serious business discussion. Each detracts from and interferes with the other.

"Power breakfasts" are a silly fad; eat breakfast before you leave home. Business lunches are expensive and needlessly time-consuming, and they can produce afternoon lethargy. Business dinners are longer and more elaborate still, and are too late in the day for serious negotiating.

Hold a business meeting before or after a meal, if you wish, but not during it.

58 Avoid holding meetings in the morning or on Friday afternoons.

For most people, the morning is the best time to do productive work. You should therefore avoid cluttering up that valuable time with meetings. Hold your meetings in the afternoon. Avoid Friday afternoon meetings, though; by then, most people are preoccupied with the upcoming weekend.

When appropriate, however, a well-run meeting can provide a good and efficient forum for exchanging thoughts and ideas. Following the suggestions in Rules 59 through 67 can help make your meetings worthwhile.

MAKE PROPER PREPARATIONS
FOR THE MEETING.

59 Distribute a written agenda before-hand to all meeting participants.

Distributing a written agenda in advance lets everyone know what will be discussed at the meeting and gives them a chance to organize their thoughts and any necessary paperwork beforehand. This saves time at the meeting itself.

If the meeting will require some background reading, also distribute the background material in advance. This will allow those attending the meeting to read the material at their own pace and to give it proper consideration.

A written agenda may not be necessary for very small, informal meetings, but the participants should always be informed of the purpose of any meeting in advance. Knowing the purpose of the meeting will give the participants a chance to prepare for it, which will make the meeting more efficient and productive.

60 Make physical arrangements for the meeting in advance.

Reserve enough space for the meeting ahead of time. Make sure that there will also be enough chairs and other necessities. Few sights are sillier than eight people arriving for a meeting in a room with five chairs and then wasting ten minutes finding and borrowing three more chairs.

61 Confirm your meeting just before you go to it.

If you are not running the meeting, take a moment to make a phone call and confirm that the meeting is still scheduled. This simple precaution can save you travel time, waiting time, and annoyance if the meeting has been canceled or postponed.

IF YOU ARE IN CHARGE OF THE MEETING, RUN IT EFFICIENTLY.

---

62 Call the meeting to order promptly.

Start the meeting on time. Don't waste the time of those who make the effort to show up on schedule. You will encourage all participants to come to your meetings on time if you show that you start meetings promptly and refuse to accommodate tardiness.

Start the meeting with an announcement that the meeting is starting. "I call this meeting to order" or "Let's begin" will get the attention of the meeting participants and make it clear that the time for premeeting chatting is over.

63 Have someone (perhaps yourself) keep minutes of the meeting.

A major meeting should have minutes, a more or less official record of the decisions reached, for the sake of clarity and future reference. You should keep your own notes of your meetings in any case. Have any minutes circulated to meeting participants afterward, and keep the minutes and your own meeting notes (if they include additional information) in the appropriate project file.

64 Keep the discussion focused and moving.

Take up one agenda item at a time, and don't let the discussion wander. Let opposing viewpoints be heard, preferably in alternation. Allow only one person at a time to speak. Discourage discussions within subgroups of participants, since these conversations ruin the cohesiveness of the meeting.

When discussion of the item at hand seems to be over, reach some conclusion on it: a decision on the substance, a decision to refer the matter elsewhere, or a decision to lay it aside. State that conclusion and then proceed to the next item.

65 Organize your comments before speaking at a meeting.

A meeting is no place for a rambling monologue. Before speaking, organize your thoughts in your head and preferably on paper. Just jot down a few key points, number them, and refer to this list. Organizing your comments saves everyone's time and creates a good impression on others.

66 At the end of the meeting, state the decisions reached and the assignments made.

A meeting is wasted if, at its conclusion, no one knows what was decided or who was supposed to do what. By summarizing the decisions and assignments, you will remind everyone of them and see whether everyone has the same understanding of them.

These decisions and assignments should be restated in writing after the meeting, in the minutes or in a memo to all participants. Keep a copy for yourself.

67 End the meeting on time.

As the meeting should begin on time, so too should it end on time. This practice accommodates the full schedules of busy people. Announce the adjournment of the meeting so that no one needs to wonder whether the meeting is over. After the meeting, leave the room at once to discourage a series of post-meeting conferences.

HANDLE PHONE CALLS
EFFICIENTLY.

68 Keep your phone calls concise.

Lengthy phone chats on the job are usually a waste of time. Before telephoning, make a list of the points you want to cover. During the call, check the points off as you complete them.

69 When you leave a phone message, include your reason for calling.

Don't just leave your name and phone number when you leave a phone message. By mentioning why you called, you give the person you called a chance to prepare for talking with you later.

Managing Your

STAFF

KEEP TRACK OF
YOUR STAFF'S ASSIGNMENTS.

---

70 Keep lists of the tasks you assign to your staff.

A list is the handiest tool for keeping track of the tasks or projects you assign to others. You should meet regularly (not necessarily frequently) with each member of your staff to review his or her projects and to check on progress and priorities.

71 Meet with your staff to exchange news and ideas.

In addition to your project-review meetings with each staff member, meet with your staff regularly as a group (assuming you manage more than one person) to impart news and invite questions or comments on ongoing organizational events or policy matters. This helps keep everyone informed and feeling like part of the team.

72 Encourage your staff to save non-urgent matters for your meeting.

Avoid a steady dribble of interruptions by having each staff member save routine queries for your regular meeting time with that staff member. This helps your staff members learn to organize their questions and to be more self-reliant by not running to you every time a minor question arises.

73 Encourage your staff to come to you with suggestions for the best use of their time at work.

Good ideas about managing time can come from anyone. Encourage your staff to bring you helpful suggestions about getting work done efficiently and effectively.

DO YOUR PART WHEN ASSIGNING TASKS.

---

74 Communicate your expectations clearly to your staff.

You must make clear your expectations about each staff member's job as a whole and about each assigned project. Be clear and consistent in your expectations. Nothing discourages a staff member more than to be given constantly shifting sets of goals and priorities.

75 Involve your staff in the planning of projects they will be carrying out.

The earlier that your staff can be involved in planning a team project, the more they will consider themselves important members of the project team, with a genuine stake in the outcome. This will improve the quantity and quality of their work.

76 Set precise objectives, but give only general guidelines for achieving them.

Your staff should be given clear, precise goals for each project. Let them work out the precise steps for achieving the goals, however. This allows scope for them to employ their intelligence and creativity and thus makes the task more interesting and the result better. Spelling out every step for them is overmanaging.

77 Assign a deadline to each project, and enforce it.

Deadlines keep projects on track toward their completion and should thus be included in any assignment. It may be helpful to set intermediate deadlines as well. Make sure each deadline is observed unless there is a very good reason for extending it.

78 Give your staff as much lead time as possible for an assignment.

This simple point is all too often overlooked. Once you have the necessary information, you should make an assignment as soon as you know you will need to. The more of a valuable resource (time) you can include with an assignment, the better the result is likely to be. Showing that you value your staff's time will encourage them to use it well.

79 Delegate responsibilities to the extent of your staff's ability.

Delegate some challenging responsibilities. Part of your job as a supervisor is to develop your people by increasing the scope of their responsibilities, thus increasing their knowledge and experience. This benefits you as well, since you thereby get better help and can accomplish more. What and how much you delegate depends on the individual abilities of your staff members, but be sure to include interesting responsibilities (challenging or not) as well as routine ones.

80 Discuss delegated responsibilities with your staff.

Delegation is not a "hit-and-run" task. Once you have decided to delegate a responsibility, ask your staff for help with it, discuss it fully, and hand over all the information you have. This helps any staff members involved to understand and participate in the new responsibility as soon and as fully as possible.

81 When you delegate a responsibility, delegate sufficient authority as well.

This obvious point is also often overlooked, which can cause much frustration. Give your staff the authority to carry out the delegated responsibility, and make this clear not only to the staff but also to those whose help the staff will need.

82 Respond calmly to mistakes made by staff members.

If a staff member bungles an assignment, don't be loud or abusive, but explain clearly and directly what the staff member did wrong and what he or she should have done instead (and therefore should do the next time).

This is a matter of common courtesy and good coaching. Everyone makes mistakes sometimes. Insulting or shouting at the person responsible for a mistake only engenders that person's resentment and defensiveness. Treat the mistake as an opportunity to learn by explaining why it was a mistake and how it should be avoided in the future.

BE A GOOD COMMUNICATOR AND A DECENT HUMAN BEING.

---

83 Keep your staff informed on matters related to their work.

No one likes to feel ignorant of what is going on. Even worse is being ignorant of matters relevant to one's job. By keeping your staff informed of relevant organizational news, you enhance morale and help them do their jobs better.

84 Treat your staff with courtesy and respect.

Courtesy should be practiced in the workplace just as every-where else. This point is all too often neglected, however, which makes too many offices the arenas of barbarians. Courtesy, including the courtesy of communication, is sur-prisingly important to the smooth operation of a workplace (as well as society at large), and it is a central theme of this and the remaining sections.

85 Thank your staff when they complete projects on time.

This is a simple example of what should be common courtesy. All people want to be appreciated for what they do. Taking the trouble to express appreciation pays rich dividends in morale.

86 If you fail a staff member in some way, admit it and apologize.

Admitting a mistake does not diminish you in your staff's eyes. On the contrary, being free enough of ego to admit errors gives you respect and credibility. The boss who thinks he or she is perfect and never acknowledges an error is generally despised.

87 Be prompt in returning phone calls or answering memos from your staff.

If you are tardy in responding to communications from your staff, they will think that you attach little importance to them and their work, and they will act accordingly. Responding promptly will also prevent your becoming a bottleneck, holding up progress on projects.

88 Do not ask your staff to come in early or to stay late unless it is necessary.

No one should be expected to devote every waking hour to the job. Your staff members have as much right to a balanced life as you have. Demanding long hours for the sake of long hours is foolish.

89 If it is necessary for your staff to come in early or to stay late, ask them to do so, and explain why.

This is a matter of clear communication of expectations and simple courtesy. Don't assume that others can read your mind and know when you want them to work extra hours.

90 If you and your staff have stayed late, tell them when they are free to leave, and thank them.

Again, this is a matter of clear communication and simple courtesy. These qualities go a long way in inspiring loyalty and getting the job done.

KEEP A POSITIVE ATTITUDE.

91 Do not complain to your staff about your boss.

Keep your complaints about your boss to yourself, or take them up with your boss privately. Complaining about your boss to your staff may make them feel that they are in your confidence, but it undermines their confidence in the organization, and this ultimately undermines morale.

92 Be enthusiastic about your work— the feeling is contagious.

Optimism and enthusiasm seep down from the top. So does pessimism. An effective leader accentuates the positive.

Managing Your

BOSS

OBSERVE THE BASICS OF A HIERARCHICAL RELATIONSHIP.

93 Carry out your boss's directives.

If you have a boss, you are in a hierarchical organization, and its fundamental operating principle is the chain of command: Those directly below carry out the directives of those directly above. The first step in managing your boss is to acknowledge, in effect, that he or she is indeed your boss.

If, for legal or moral reasons, you feel that you cannot obey a directive, tell your boss so and explain why. If your boss then refuses to withdraw the directive, resign and find another job.

94 Treat your boss with respect and courtesy but not with obsequiousness.

Treat everyone, including your boss, with respect and courtesy in and out of the office. Do not fawn over your superiors, though; obsequiousness will erode your self-respect, the respect of your colleagues, and even the respect of the boss you are seeking to please. If your boss is so egotistical or insecure as to require obsequious fawning, find yourself another boss as soon as possible.

95 Report to your boss regularly on the status of major projects.

Keep your boss informed. That helps your boss to manage the delegated work properly and to share accordingly in the responsibility for your projects.

HELP YOUR BOSS
BE YOUR MANAGER.

---

96 Report to your boss promptly any serious problems in any of your projects.

The timely reporting of problems is an important part of communicating with your boss, who then will have as much lead time as possible to help solve the problem. Especially avoid taking your boss by surprise when you must miss a major deadline.

97 Suggest ways in which your special strengths could be put to use.

You know best what your special strengths and talents are. Think of ways to apply them to your job, and suggest these applications to your boss. Using your abilities in varied and creative ways will make you more useful on the job, will help you to enjoy your work more, and will impress your boss with your initiative.

DEAL WITH PROBLEMS IN A STRAIGHTFORWARD MANNER.

---

98 Be frank with your boss, but keep any criticisms technical or procedural.

Honest communication is the hallmark of the best working relationships. There may be times when you must point out to your boss perceived flaws in organizational operations or other matters, including some for which your boss is responsible. At such times, offer your analysis, but focus on technical or procedural flaws rather than personal shortcomings. Be sure to propose a possible solution.

99 If your boss mismanages you, suggest how you might work better together.

If you find that your boss doesn't manage you in the way that a boss should manage his or her staff (see previous section, Managing Your Staff), suggest corrective changes that will enable the two of you to work better together.

Often this may involve opening or enhancing lines of communication between you and your boss, perhaps by meeting more regularly to review current projects or relevant organizational news. Be careful to phrase suggestions constructively rather than critically. For example, say, "I think I'd do better with the assignment if we could meet weekly to discuss it" rather than "You need to meet with me more often."

100 Do not complain about your boss to others in the workplace.

The effects of complaining to your staff are discussed in Rule 91. Complaining about your boss to others in the workplace, whether they are on your staff or not, is not only bad form, it also can be very risky and counterproductive. Word gets around an office very quickly, and the effect of dissension on morale can be very destructive. There is also a good chance that word of your complaining will get back to your boss, which can jeopardize your own standing.

Take up complaints with your boss directly, as described in Rules 98 and 99. If afterward you still must grumble, grumble at home.

Managing Your

COLLEAGUES

---

*BE HELPFUL
AND FAIR TO OTHERS.*

---

101 Be honest and straightforward with your colleagues.

Earn a reputation for personal integrity. If no one can believe what you say, you will get nowhere (outside of politics, anyway!). Also, as someone has said, telling the truth is easier on the memory as well as on the conscience.

102 Treat your colleagues with respect and courtesy.

This is, of course, the way you should treat everyone. Respectful, courteous behavior will also encourage the same in others. Like most of the "obvious" rules in this book, this one is often neglected. You can do at least your part to encourage civility in the workplace and elsewhere.

103 Keep your colleagues informed on the parts of your work that affect them.

Let your colleagues know about progress on projects of yours that will affect their work. This will help them to achieve their goals and to understand the value of your work. They may also have valuable insights or suggestions to offer.

104 Keep phone calls and visits friendly but to the point during business hours.

Friendly chats in the office, when longer than a few minutes or so, become a waste of valuable time. Don't fool yourself into writing the time off as "networking." (You can be sure that your boss won't be fooled!)

105 Be cautious about developing personal friendships with colleagues.

Personal relationships can get messy in the office, especially when they involve romance. Be cordial to your colleagues, but develop your deeper relationships outside the office.

106 Let your colleagues know when you want to be left undisturbed.

As discussed in Rule 2, it may be convenient for you to set some time aside to work undisturbed on major projects, on either a regular or an occasional basis. When you do, inform your colleagues in advance so that they will not disturb you during that time. The advance notice may be brief, but it will give your colleagues a chance to ask a quick question or impart any urgent information before you sequester yourself.

107 Go to experts for needed information.

Learn what special areas of knowledge or expertise your colleagues have, and take advantage of their knowledge when you need it. Going to an expert is usually much quicker than doing the research yourself. Naturally, you should reciprocate whenever they request similar help from you.

108 Ask for help in achieving your goals.

None of us can achieve all our goals, in or out of the office, without help. When you need a colleague's help, ask for it, and give help when it is asked of you.

109 Involve your colleagues in every stage of planning a team project.

This gives you the benefit of their ideas and gives them a greater interest in the success of the project. What works for your staff (see Rule 75) can work for your colleagues as well.

110 Share the credit for accomplishments.

When others help you to accomplish a goal, acknowledge this and thank them. They will appreciate the recognition and will be all the more willing to help you again in the future. No one likes or respects someone who "hogs" the credit. For true achievers, there is enough credit to go around.

Lists and Files

LISTS

Personal Goals (*#36*)

Professional Goals (*#36*)

Things To Do This Year (*#40*)

Things To Do This Month (*#40*)

Things To Do This Week (*#40*)

Things To Do Today (*#3, 40*)

Appointment Calendar (*#5*)

Daily Schedule (*#1*)

Projects List (*#41*)

Project Steps (*#44*)

Pending Reading (*#34*)

Reference Material (*#33*)

Time Log (*#7*)

Achievements List (*#51*)

FILES

Reminder File (*#5*)

Project File (*#26*)

Pending Reading (*#34*)

Reference Material (*#33*)

Permanent, or Subject, Files (*#26*)

Reminder Chart

Controlling Your Day,

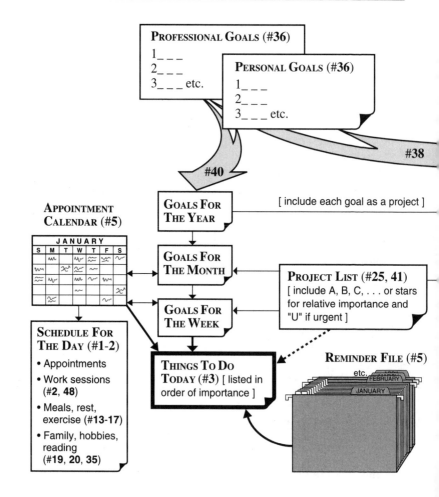

PROFESSIONAL GOALS (#36)
1_ _ _
2_ _ _
3_ _ _ etc.

PERSONAL GOALS (#36)
1_ _ _
2_ _ _
3_ _ _ etc.

#38

#40

APPOINTMENT
CALENDAR (#5)

GOALS FOR
THE YEAR

[include each goal as a project]

JANUARY

S	M	T	W	T	F	S

GOALS FOR
THE MONTH

PROJECT LIST (#25, 41)
[include A, B, C, . . . or stars
for relative importance and
"U" if urgent]

GOALS FOR
THE WEEK

SCHEDULE FOR
THE DAY (#1-2)

- Appointments
- Work sessions
  (#2, 48)
- Meals, rest,
  exercise (#13-17)
- Family, hobbies,
  reading
  (#19, 20, 35)

THINGS TO DO
TODAY (#3) [listed in
order of importance]

REMINDER FILE (#5)

etc. FEBRUARY
JANUARY

Paperwork, and Projects

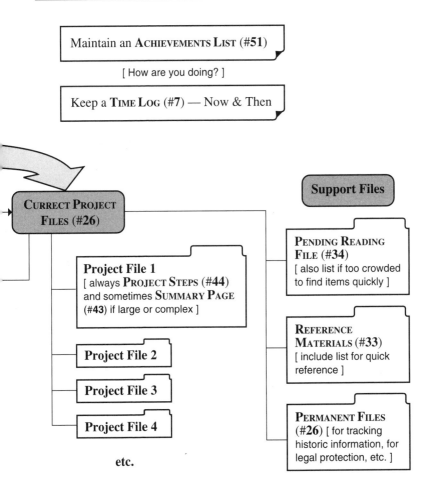

Maintain an ACHIEVEMENTS LIST (#51)

[How are you doing?]

Keep a TIME LOG (#7) — Now & Then

CURRECT PROJECT FILES (#26)

Support Files

Project File 1
[always PROJECT STEPS (#44) and sometimes SUMMARY PAGE (#43) if large or complex]

Project File 2

Project File 3

Project File 4

etc.

PENDING READING FILE (#34)
[also list if too crowded to find items quickly]

REFERENCE MATERIALS (#33)
[include list for quick reference]

PERMANENT FILES (#26) [for tracking historic information, for legal protection, etc.]

The Sacred Rules of Management

Summary

MANAGING YOUR DAY

Plan your day, and put your plan on paper.

1. Write down a schedule for your day.
2. Include some prime working time and some quiet time in your schedule.
3. Write down a Things to Do list for your day.
4. Work your way down each list in order, checking off each event or task as you complete it.
5. Keep an appointment calendar, lists of goals, and a Reminder File.
6. Follow a regular schedule on weekdays.
7. Keep a time log occasionally.

Get through the routine chores of the day quickly and efficiently.

8. Reduce your commuting time as much as possible, and put it to good use.
9. Consolidate your routine chores.
10. Do chores and errands at unusual times.
11. Consolidate your errands into a single trip.
12. Take advantage of pockets of available time.

Take care of your health for a full life.

13. Eat sensibly.

14. Don't drink alcohol during the working day.

15. Exercise regularly.

16. Take an afternoon nap.

17. Get enough sleep at night.

Lead a balanced life.

18. Limit your vocational work to eight hours a day.

19. Spend time with your family and friends.

20. Cultivate outside interests and hobbies.

21. Plan your weekend—and stay away from your office.

MANAGING YOUR PAPERWORK

Do business in writing.

22. Keep notes of ideas, conversations, and decisions.

23. Date your documents.

24. Always have a notepad handy.

Make good use of file folders.

25. Keep lists of projects instead of piles of paper.

26. Keep a file for each project or job-related subject.

27. Clear your desk of all papers except those you are working on at the moment.

28. When you complete a project, purge and relocate its file.

29. Periodically conduct a major purge of your files.

Learn to process your incoming paperwork efficiently.

30. Sort through your in-box two or three times a day.

31. Sort through your in-box efficiently.

32. Reply promptly to memos and letters.

Organize your reading and reference material.

33. Keep your reference material in an appropriately labeled file folder or a binder.

34. Keep a file of your reading matter.

35. Schedule regular reading time.

MANAGING YOUR PROJECTS

Get your goals down on paper.

36. List your long-term personal and professional goals.

37. Make your goals specific and concrete, and rank them.

38. Treat each goal as a project.

39. Review your goals periodically.

40. List goals for each year, month, week, and day.

Use lists and notes to organize and keep track of projects at the office.

41. Keep a prioritized, running list of current projects.

42. Eliminate projects that do not belong to you.

43. Write a summary of each project you take on.

44. Prepare a Project Steps list.

45. Work your way down the list of Project Steps.

Manage your project time well.

46. Develop your powers of concentration.

47. Allocate enough time to complete the project on schedule.

48. Schedule reasonably long, uninterrupted blocks of time to work on important projects.

49. When traveling, take books or project papers with you.

50. Try to finish projects just in time—on time, but not by much.

Make notes on your completed projects.

51. Keep an Achievements List of professional accomplishments.

52. If the completed project will recur, note and file any lessons you learned in completing it.

Meet crises calmly and directly.

53. When a crisis arises, stay calm and think the problem through.

54. Sleep on important decisions.

55. Don't procrastinate.

MANAGING YOUR MEETINGS

Choose your meetings carefully.

56. Avoid unnecessary meetings.

57. Don't meet for a meal to discuss business.

58. Avoid holding meetings in the morning or on Friday afternoons.

Make proper preparations for the meeting.

59. Distribute a written agenda beforehand to all meeting participants.

60. Make physical arrangements for the meeting in advance.

61. Confirm your meeting just before you go to it.

If you are in charge of the meeting, run it efficiently.

62. Call the meeting to order promptly.

63. Have someone (perhaps yourself) keep minutes of the meeting.

64. Keep the discussion focused and moving.

65. Organize your comments before speaking at a meeting.

66. At the end of the meeting, state the decisions reached and the assignments made.

67. End the meeting on time.

Handle phone calls efficiently.

68. Keep your phone calls concise.

69. When you leave a phone message, include your reason for calling.

MANAGING YOUR STAFF

Keep track of your staff's assignments.

70. Keep lists of the tasks you assign to your staff.

71. Meet with your staff to exchange news and ideas.

72. Encourage your staff to save nonurgent matters for your meeting.

73. Encourage your staff to come to you with suggestions for the best use of their time at work.

Do your part when assigning tasks.

74. Communicate your expectations clearly to your staff.

75. Involve your staff in the planning of projects they will be carrying out.

76. Set precise objectives, but give only general guidelines for achieving them.

77. Assign a deadline to each project, and enforce it.

78. Give your staff as much lead time as possible for an assignment.

79. Delegate responsibilities to the extent of your staff's ability.

80. Discuss delegated responsibilities with your staff.

81. When you delegate a responsibility, delegate sufficient authority as well.

82. Respond calmly to mistakes made by staff members.

Be a good communicator and a decent human being.

83. Keep your staff informed on matters related to their work.

84. Treat your staff with courtesy and respect.

85. Thank your staff when they complete projects on time.

86. If you fail a staff member in some way, admit it and apologize.

87. Be prompt in returning phone calls or answering memos from your staff.

88. Do not ask your staff to come in early or to stay late unless it is necessary.

89. If it is necessary for your staff to come in early or to stay late, ask them to do so, and explain why.

90. If you and your staff have stayed late, tell them when they are free to leave, and thank them.

Keep a positive attitude.

91. Do not complain to your staff about your boss.

92. Be enthusiastic about your work—the feeling is contagious.

MANAGING YOUR BOSS

Observe the basics of a hierarchical relationship.

93. Carry out your boss's directives.

94. Treat your boss with respect and courtesy but not with obsequiousness.

95. Report to your boss regularly on the status of major projects.

Help your boss be your manager.

96. Report to your boss promptly any serious problems in any of your projects.

97. Suggest ways in which your special strengths could be put to use.

Deal with problems in a straightforward manner.

98. Be frank with your boss, but keep any criticisms technical or procedural.

99. If your boss mismanages you, suggest how you might work better together.

100. Do not complain about your boss to others in the workplace.

MANAGING YOUR COLLEAGUES

Be helpful and fair to others.

101. Be honest and straightforward with your colleagues.

102. Treat your colleagues with respect and courtesy.

103. Keep your colleagues informed on parts of your work that affect them.

104. Keep phone calls and visits friendly but to the point during business hours.

105. Be cautious about developing personal friendships with colleagues.

106. Let your colleagues know when you want to be left undisturbed.

107. Go to experts for needed information.

108. Ask for help in achieving your goals.

109. Involve your colleagues in every stage of planning a team project.

110. Share the credit for accomplishments.

Index